FREMDSPRACHENTEXTE · ENGLISCH

Urban Legends

Ausgewählt und herausgegeben
von Heike Jüngst

Mit 15 Illustrationen
von David Austin

Reclam

RECLAMS UNIVERSAL-BIBLIOTHEK Nr. 9065

Gesamtherstellung: Reclam, Ditzingen. Printed in Germany 2015

ISBN 978-3-15-009065-7

www.reclam.de

Inhalt

Vorwort

Urban legends sind überall, man muß nur die Augen offenhalten. Ob sie mündlich weitererzählt werden, oder ob man sie in Form eines Zeitungsartikels findet, ob der Wahrheitsgehalt bestätigt oder angezweifelt wird: wir sind von *urban legends* umgeben. Auch der Bekanntheitsgrad, den das Genre heute erreicht hat, konnte nicht verhindern, daß in den letzten Monaten Geschichten über Mäuseskelette in Schokoriegeln die Runde durch englische Zeitungen machten. Ebenfalls in England fand sich in diesem Jahr die hübsche Geschichte von der handtellergroßen Kröte in der Tüte mit vorgewaschenem Salat. Unnötig zu erwähnen, daß es mir trotz großer Anstrengung bisher nicht gelungen ist, eine solche Salattüte zu finden.
Die Wissenschaft beschäftigt sich etwa seit den vierziger Jahren intensiv mit *urban legends*. Die Gattung selbst ist alt, denn im Grunde genommen sind *urban legends* einfach Volkssagen. Viele Sagen leben heute als *urban legends* weiter; viele der sonderbaren Begebenheiten aus Hebels *Rheinländischem Hausfreund* (1808–11) ähneln in Struktur und Inhalt den *urban legends*.
Urban legend, contemporary legend, urban myth, moderne Großstadtsage – all diese Gattungsbezeichnungen beziehen sich auf das Gleiche: eine Geschichte von zweifelhafter Glaubwürdigkeit und sagenhaftem Inhalt, die so weitererzählt wird, als sei sie tatsächlich passiert,[1] und zwar gerade eben dem »friend of a

1 Vgl. Rolf Wilhelm Brednich, *Die Spinne in der Yucca-Palme*, München: Beck, 1990, S. 6: »[. . .] unter Sagen verstehen wir mündlich überlieferte

friend«, kurz: »foaf«,[2] dem Bekannten eines Bekannten.

Urban legends werden in den verschiedensten Situationen von den verschiedensten Menschen erzählt.[3] Besonders beliebt sind sie im Zeltlager oder Landschulheim, aber auch im täglichen Arbeitsleben begegnet uns die eine oder andere *urban legend*. Als wesentlicher Bestandteil von Klatsch und Tratsch erfüllen sie eine wichtige soziale Funktion, einerseits durch ihren kommunikativen Charakter, andererseits durch die Inhalte:

> »Moderne Sagen, so läßt sich resümieren, stellen sich bei näherer Betrachtung als ein Ausdruck von Ideen, Gefühlen, Befürchtungen und vor allem von Sorgen, Nöten und Ängsten der heutigen Zeit heraus.«[4]

Auch außerhalb der mündlichen und schriftlichen Überlieferung begegnen uns *urban legends* auf Schritt und Tritt: in Werbespots und Filmen zum Beispiel.[5] Es spricht für die Popularität von *urban legends*, daß gerade solche Werbespots häufig mit Preisen ausgezeichnet werden. Die Geschichte, die in dieser Auswahl unter »Not Your Lucky Night« erscheint, hat große Ähn-

Erzählungen und Berichte von außergewöhnlichen Erlebnissen, Ereignissen oder Erscheinungen, die mit dem Anspruch auf Glaubwürdigkeit erzählt werden.«

2 »The storytellers assume that the true facts of each case lie just one or two informants back down the line with a reliable witness, or in a news media report« (Jan Harold Brunvand, *The Vanishing Hitchhiker: American Urban Legends and Their Meanings*, New York: Norton, 1981, S. xi).

3 Vgl. ebd.: »They are an integral part of white Anglo-American culture and are told and believed by some of the most sophisticated ›folk‹ of modern society – young people, urbanites, and the well educated.«

4 R. W. Brednich, *Die Spinne in der Yucca-Palme*, S. 18 f.

5 Vgl. ebd., S. 13 passim.

lichkeit mit einem Werbespot der norwegischen Fluglinie Braathens. Dort entkleidet sich der Ehemann im Flur, um vor seiner Frau ein erotisches Tänzchen aufzuführen; leider sieht er sich plötzlich auch mit seinen Schwiegereltern konfrontiert, die er zuvor durchs Schlüsselloch nicht sehen konnte.

Oft kann man nicht mehr sagen, ob die *urban legend* den Film inspiriert hat oder ob umgekehrt aus der Geschichte im Film eine *urban legend* entstanden ist. Die Geschichte vom »Hare Drier« in der vorliegenden Sammlung paßte großartig in den Film »Nach fünf im Urwald« (Regie: Hans-Christian Schmid, Deutschland 1996). Die *legend* vom ausgegrabenen und gewaschenen Hasen wird hier ganz bewußt eingesetzt, um den spießigen Nachbarn, dem der Hase gehört, zu charakterisieren. Sie wird erweitert, indem die altkluge Tochter den Vater und einen Bekannten beim Waschen und Fönen des toten Hasen beobachtet und das Ganze als düsteres Ritual interpretiert. Auch die Reaktion des Nachbarn: »Erwin ist auferstanden!«, in der er die Weiße und Reinheit des Fells preist, weist auf eine religiöse Einbettung hin (aber auch auf das weiße Weiß der deutschen Waschmittelreklame). Das Erkennen der Geschichte als *urban legend* durch das Publikum ist dabei geplant. Es handelt sich um einen Rückgriff auf gemeinsame kulturelle Kenntnisse. Schließlich wurde mit *Düstere Legenden* (*Urban Legends*, USA 1998, Regie: Jamie Blanks) ein Teenie-Horror-Film gedreht, in dem Verbrechen nach dem Muster bekannter *urban legends* verübt werden.

Auch in der Kinderliteratur finden wir *urban legends*. »The Performing Elephant«, ursprünglich ein englischer Text, war in den siebziger Jahren als »Der Elefant auf Papas Auto« von David Henry Wilson ein beliebter Vorlesetext.[6] Er ist noch heute eine der schönsten literarischen Fassungen einer *urban legend*.

Urban legends stehen trotz ihrer weltweiten Verbreitung in bestimmten landeskundlichen Traditionen. Das erleichtert die Glaubwürdigkeit – je mehr Details vertraut erscheinen, desto eher glaubt man auch das Unglaubliche.

Liest man *urban legends* aus anderen Kulturen, so kann man ihnen vielfältige Informationen über deren Alltag, Erzähltraditionen und Moralvorstellungen entnehmen.[7] So sind in den USA *urban legends* ein beliebter Party-Erzählstoff an Colleges. Die hier unter dem Stichwort »Teenage Horror Stories« versammelten *legends* setzen Kenntnisse über die amerikanische Lebensweise voraus, z. B. daß Doppelzimmer im Studentenwohnheim nicht ungewöhnlich sind. Babysitting spielt eine viel wichtigere Rolle als in Deutschland, da viele Mädchen sich damit einen Teil des Geldes für den Collegebesuch verdienen und nicht einfach nur ihr Taschengeld aufbessern. Autos sind in den USA durch die größeren Entfernungen besonders wichtig, obwohl Europa da aufgeholt hat. In den USA kann man aber bereits mit sechzehn Jahren den Führerschein machen, und das Rendezvous im Auto als von den Eltern nicht überwachter Freiraum hat eine größere Bedeutung und Tradition als bei uns.

Wie unverwüstlich *urban legends* sind, zeigt die Tatsa-

6 Abgedruckt in: Gertraud Middelhauve (Hrsg.), *Dichter Europas erzählen Kindern*, München: dtv, 1975, S. 39–42.

7 Vgl. dazu auch Brednich, S. 19.

che, daß auch das Internet nicht von ihnen verschont bleibt. Läßt man in aller Unschuld eine Internet-Suchmaschine mit dem Stichwort »Cookies« eine Suche starten, so erhält man nicht nur die gewünschten Backrezepte oder Programmiertips, sondern eine Unzahl von Beiträgen, die sich mit den Neiman-Marcus-Cookies beschäftigen (die gleiche Geschichte, die hier unter dem Titel »The Mrs. Fields Cookie Recipe« erscheint). Man erhält verschiedene Textversionen der *urban legend* selbst, oft erweitert um einen empörten Kommentar, an dieser Firma müsse aber dringend Rache geübt werden.[8] Andere Websites sind aufgeklärter und outen die Geschichte als *urban legend.* Das Rezept selbst bekommt man natürlich auch, allerdings in vielen verschiedenen Varianten.[9] Sogar Internet-Handbücher weisen auf den *legend*-Taumel im Netz hin und warnen davor.[10]
Die *urban legends* in dieser Sammlung sollen vor allem Lesegenuß bieten: kurze, relativ einfache Stücke auf englisch, mit schaurig-schönem Inhalt.

Heike Jüngst

8 Vgl. dazu Rolf Wilhelm Brednich, *Die Ratte am Strohhalm*, München: Beck, 1996, S. 34 f.

9 Siehe dazu auch J. H. Brunvand, *The Vanishing Hitchhiker*, S. 219 ff., der beschreibt, wie dieses Verfahren außerhalb des Internet mit Fotokopien abläuft.

10 Empfehlenswert zum Nachlesen: Tracy LaQuey, *The European Internet Companion*, Wokingham [u. a.]: Addison-Wesley, 1995.

PUSSY

Pets and Other Animals

The Persian Cat and the Chihuahua

A lady, who lived down the road from a friend of mine, owned a beautiful Persian cat. She had been thinking of buying a puppy as a second pet and, on visiting the pet shop, decided upon a Chihuahua. She carried the tiny creature home very carefully, fed it and, when she went to bed later that evening, left it in the kitchen with the Persian cat.

The next morning, when she went down to the kitchen, the cat was lying there looking very contented but she could not find the puppy anywhere. She searched in every room of the house but not a trace of the dog could be found. While considering what to do next about the missing animal, she bent down to pick up the cat's bowl in order to feed it. To her horror, there in the bowl was some fur and a few small bones – all that remained of the Chihuahua. The Persian cat had eaten the puppy mistaking it for a rat.

2 **Persian cat:** Perserkatze (Rassekatze).
Chihuahua: kleinste Hunderasse.
5 **puppy:** Welpe.

The Performing Elephant

Bill's car, a Mini, had recently been involved in an accident and he had just had it resprayed bright red. Heading for town he was surprised by the number of people about – he had forgotten that it was the day the big circus parade was due to pass through.

Parking in the main street, Bill went to do his weekend shopping. Shortly afterwards the circus parade came into view. There were the clowns, acrobats, horses, a brass band and, at the rear of the procession, a large performing elephant.

One of the tricks the elephant had been taught to do was, when the band played a particular tune, to rear up in the air and, standing on his hind legs, turn in a full circle. The trick then culminated with the elephant sitting down on a large drum painted bright red.

The elephant had just drawn level with Bill's Mini when the bandmaster, for no particular reason, instructed the musicians to strike up the tune for this trick. Up in the air went the elephant, round and round it went, then, as it always did, it sat on the nearby bright red object – unfortunately, in this instance it proved to be Bill's freshly painted car.

13 **to rear up:** sich auf die Hinterbeine stellen.
14 **hind legs:** Hinterbeine.
15 **to culminate:** (fig.) gipfeln, den Höhepunkt finden.
18 **bandmaster:** Kapellmeister.

Notes

This delightful, and highly credible, legend has been circulating in Europe for at least the past twenty years. While told in England about a Mini, in Europe other makes of popular small car, such as Volkswagen and Fiat, suffer the same indignity. At one time the legend was so popular that a garage in Sweden, as a stunt, had publicity photographs taken of an elephant sitting on a Volkswagen.

2 **credible:** glaubwürdig.
to circulate: im Umlauf sein.
5 **indignity:** Entwürdigung.
6 **stunt:** Werbegag.

[Illustration] **Moore:** Henry M. (1898–1986), englischer Bildhauer, dessen Skulpturen oft abstrakte menschliche Formen mit großen Löchern darstellen.

Woodworm-infested Shoes

Some years ago a massive campaign was launched advertising shoes with wooden non-breakable heels – much better than the breakable plastic heels, it was claimed. Unfortunately, the manufacturers overlooked treating the shoes against woodworm and once the worms got into the heels they just ate them all away and the heels disintegrated, broke up and snapped off.

1 **woodworm-infested:** vom Holzwurm befallen.
2 **to launch a campaign:** eine (Werbe-)Kampagne starten.
3 **non-breakable:** unzerbrechlich.
8 **to disintegrate:** zerfallen.
to snap off: abbrechen.

The Girl with the Beehive Hairdo

A girl managed to wrap her hair into a perfect beehive. Proud of her accomplishment, she kept spraying it and spraying it, never bothering to wash it again. Bugs began to live in her hair. After about six months, they ate through to her brain and killed her.

MORAL: wash your hair or die.

1 **beehive hairdo:** Bienenkorbfrisur; hochtoupierte Frisur, wie sie in den fünfziger Jahren modern war (*beehive:* Bienenkorb).
4 **bugs:** Ungeziefer, Insekten.

The Dead Cat in the Package

Chamber of Commerce Manager Jules Hendricks tells about a neighbor of his in Indianapolis who found a novel way of disposing of the remains of a dead cat. Knowing the city ordinance prohibited burying the body, the woman called a friend of hers who lived in the country and asked if she would bury the body for her. The friend agreed, and they planned to meet for the exchange at a downtown department store tea room.

Carrying the cat in a brown paper bag, the woman stopped to do some shopping en route to her rendezvous – and carelessly laid the bag on a counter. When she returned, the bag was gone. A clerk sympathized, explaining that the store had been having trouble with shoplifters lately. Her problem solved (if not in the way she had planned), the woman started home.

Just outside the store, she found a crowd of people had gathered. Squeezing among them to find out what the attraction was, she saw the unconscious body of a 200-pound woman, clutching to her breast a brown paper bag from which protruded the head of her dead cat.

5 **city ordinance:** Gemeindeverordnung.
9 f. **tea room:** Café.
12 **en route:** unterwegs.
14 **to sympathize:** sein Mitleid ausdrücken.
16 **shoplifter:** Ladendieb.
21 **to clutch s.th. to one's breast:** etwas umklammern, an die Brust pressen.
22 **to protrude:** herausragen.

The Cat Parcel

She is a maiden-lady scholar and was working at the British Museum. Living in a boarding house, she was unable to keep a cat to fend off loneliness, but an English friend offered her one, which, the friend suggested, she might secrete in her room; she would have to tip the maid with some silence money, but the cat was well-behaved – a box in the bathroom with some newspapers would do. So, she brought the cat to her room, under her coat, and had it for company during the winter. But presently the cat died. So she had to dispose of it. She made up a neat little bundle and was about to put it into the incinerator when the proprietress greeted her. "This will never do," she said to herself, and went off to the library. On the way, she passed a likely-looking place to ditch the cat, a culvert or something, but this time a bobby came around the corner just in time to deter her – she thought he might ask

2 **maiden-lady:** unverheiratete Frau, ‚altes Mädchen'.
4 **to fend off s.th.:** gegen etwas ankämpfen.
6 **to secrete:** verstecken.
7 **to tip s.o. with some silence money:** jdm. Geld zustecken, damit er, sie nichts ausplaudert.
8 **well-behaved:** gut erzogen.
11 **presently** (adv.): kurz darauf.
12 **bundle:** Bündel.
13 **incinerator:** Verbrennungsofen.
13 f. **proprietress:** Hausbesitzerin.
16 **likely-looking:** passend.
culvert: Kanal.
17 **bobby:** Bobby, englischer Polizist.
18 **to deter:** abhalten.

questions. On her way to lunch, the guard called to her to tell her that she'd forgotten her parcel. "This is getting to be funny," she said to herself. But she resolved on taking a bus ride and leaving the cat on it. But as she rose to leave, a passenger tipped his hat and handed her her forgotten parcel. She tried to leave it at the restaurant where she ate lunch. But here the waitress prevented her. And again she was foiled on a subway ride. Just about desperate, she phoned the friend who had given her the cat. "Bring it out," the friend said, "and we'll take it to the pet cemetery in the neighborhood." So she did. When she got there, she thought she'd take one last look at her beloved cat and opened the parcel. It was a leg of mutton!

1 **guard:** Aufseher.
8 **to foil s.o.:** jdm. einen Strich durch die Rechnung machen.
subway: U-Bahn (AE). Die Geschichte spielt zwar in London, wird aber von einem Amerikaner erzählt.
11 **pet cemetery:** Tierfriedhof.
14 **leg of mutton:** Hammelkeule.

The Snake in the Sweater

This happened to my girlfriend's sister-in-law. One day she was shopping at Klein's Department Store in Greenbelt (Maryland). She saw some sweaters that were on sale and tried some on. She felt this prick on her arm but thought it was just the tag. Anyway, she continued shopping. Later in the day her arm started itching. It swelled up and got real red. By evening she felt faint. Her husband took her to hospital where she was listed in serious or critical condition. They completely retraced her steps that day to try and find out what happened to her. Come to find out it was from that prick from the sweaters. The sweaters had been imported from Japan. Somehow a snake got into them and started a nest. The eggs had hatched and there were little tiny snakes in some of the sweaters.

6 **tag:** Preisschild.
10 **to be listed in serious condition:** als ernster Fall eingestuft werden, schwerkrank sein.
11 **to retrace s.o.'s steps:** Schritt für Schritt zurückverfolgen, was jd. getan hat.
15 **to hatch:** ausbrüten.

There was this Snake, See ...

"I'd like some information," a male caller told the Dallas News City Desk some weeks ago.

It seems he'd heard about a woman who had gone to a local discount store to look at some fur coats imported from Mexico. When the woman put her hand in the coat pocket, she felt a sudden, sharp pain. A few minutes later her arm supposedly had started turning black and blue.

"Well," the man continued, "they rushed her to the hospital. It seems that pain was a snake in the coat pocket. The woman's arm had to be amputated."

The reporter said he'd check the story.

About that time a woman called with the same story, only she'd heard the woman died right in Presbyterian Hospital's emergency ward.

Presbyterian Hospital said it had no such case on record.

"My brother is a doctor," another caller explained. "He's on the staff at Baylor Hospital and he was present when they brought the woman in."

Baylor Hospital said it also had no such case on record. Neither did the police or the health department.

2 **caller:** Anrufer; Besucher.
2 f. **Dallas News:** Name einer Zeitung.
3 **city desk** (AE): Lokalredaktion.
8 **supposedly** (adv.): angeblich.
16 **emergency ward:** Notaufnahme.
23 **health department:** Gesundheitsamt.

The doctor was questioned, he said it wasn't actually he who was present but a friend.
The friend explained he wasn't present either, he had just overheard two nurses talking about it.
After about 10 calls from other "interested" persons the fur coat turned into some material that had come in from India. A man gave the name of the insurance company which was handling the case.
The insurance man said it wasn't actually his company but his next door neighbor's cousin's company.
The story spread through the city and seemed to be the main topic of conversation at cocktail parties and bridge games.
Finally a caller came up with the victim's name.
The News called and the "victim" answered the phone. She said she had never been in better health. Someone must have had her confused with someone else, but she had heard the rumor. Only she heard the snake was found in a basket of fruit.
The neighbor's cousin's insurance company was located.
He said the only snake bite victim he knew of was his daughter and that had happened on a family hike the summer before.
The managers of the two discount stores most frequently mentioned in the rumor said the story is one that has been traveling across the country. Both noted that neither store even sells fur coats.
The doctor who was actually supposed to have per-

4 **to overhear:** zufällig mitanhören.
6 **material:** Stoff.

formed the surgery said he was a pediatrician and never did surgery.

"But as long as I've got you on the phone," he explained, "I'd like to ask you about something else. It seems a story going around about a young girl who got blood poisoning from a certain kind of spray net that's on the market . . .!"

1 **pediatrician:** Kinderarzt.
6 **blood poisoning:** Blutvergiftung.
spray net: Haarspray.

A Bug in the Ear

In the most common modern version of the story, a woman is lying on a beach, when a tiny earwig slips into her ear and crawls straight ahead as far as possible. The woman leaves the beach unawares. But several days later, she suffers an intense earache, and goes to a doctor for an examination.

"Hmmm. He's too far in to grab," the doctor says. "We'll just have to wait. He'll work his way through and come out the other side."

But the doctor has made a big mistake. Weeks later, when the insect emerges from the woman's other ear, the "he" bug turns out to be a "she." So the doctor offers a revised opinion. "I'm afraid this female earwig may have laid eggs in your head. If so, they'll hatch and eventually eat out your brain."

1 **bug:** Käfer, Insekt.
3 **earwig:** Ohrkriecher, -laus, -wurm.
5 **unawares** (adv.): ohne etwas zu ahnen.
6 **earache:** Ohrenschmerzen.
13 f. **the doctor offers a revised opinion:** der Arzt revidiert seine Diagnose.
15 **to hatch:** schlüpfen.

Not My Dog

A woman is invited to call at the home of a woman who is wealthier than she is (or, in variations, older or socially superior). From the moment she is invited, the caller is unsure about how to behave – how to sit, how to take tea, etc. And matters are made worse when the time of the visit arrives. A large, lively, dirty beast of a dog is sitting in the front yard, and when the hostess welcomes the caller into the house, the dog follows her inside. While the caller tries to respect the social amenities, that darn dog does not. It tracks mud about the room, sniffs the cookies, and paws the furniture. The caller makes small talk, but the conversation becomes strained. Still, both parties keep a stiff upper lip, observing proper etiquette.

Finally the visit comes to an end. As the caller rises to leave, the hostess, with one eye on the wreckage, remarks icily, "And don't forget to take your dog!"

"My dog?" the caller says. "I thought it was yours!"

5 **caller:** Besucher.
6 **to take tea:** Tee trinken.
8 **front yard:** Vorgarten (AE).
10 f. **social amenities** (pl.): Etikette.
11 **darn** (slang): verflixt.
11 f. **to track mud about the room:** im ganzen Zimmer Schmutzspuren hinterlassen.
12 **to sniff s.th.:** an etwas schnüffeln.
to paw s.th.: die Pfoten auf etwas legen, etwas betatschen.
14 **strained:** gezwungen.
to keep a stiff upper lip: sich nichts anmerken lassen.
17 **wreckage:** Trümmerfeld, Chaos.

The Hare Drier

As far as urban legends went, 1988 was the Year of the Rabbit – or at least it included the Season of the Rabbit. The hottest story going around that spring and summer was one about a dead rabbit that got blow-dried. I dubbed the legend "The Hare Drier." (Yes, I know there's a difference between hares and rabbits, but the pun was irresistible.)

The usual story goes about like this: One day a woman is horrified to see her dog holding a dead rabbit in its mouth. Her neighbors have always kept a pet rabbit in a cage behind the house, and she recognizes the dead animal as their pet. The woman takes the rabbit from her dog, cleans it up as best she can, blow-dries its fur, and – her neighbors being gone – sneaks into their yard and replaces the restored rabbit in its cage in a lifelike posture. The next day, she sees a police car parked in front of her neighbor's house. Curious, she goes outside and asks what's going on. "A nuisance call," the officer

1 **hare drier:** Wortspiel mit *hair drier* ›Fön‹ (*hare:* Hase).
5 f. **to blow-dry:** fönen.
6 **to dub:** nennen.
8 **pun:** Wortspiel.
irresistible: unwiderstehlich.
15 **to sneak:** schleichen.
yard: Garten (AE).
16 **lifelike:** lebensecht.
17 **posture:** Haltung, Positur.
19 **nuisance call:** hier: Fehlalarm.

says. "Their pet rabbit died yesterday, and some weirdo dug it up and put it back in its cage."
If you haven't heard this one yet, you must lead a sheltered life.

1 **weirdo:** Spinner.

Dangers of the Microwave Oven II

I once heard of an elderly lady who used to breed pedigree cats and exhibit them at shows. She specialized in Persian cats and their long hair always made it a difficult task to clean and groom them for showing. In order to cut down the effort involved the old lady had evolved the practice of first washing the cat, towelling it dry and then, finally, giving it a very brief warming in her electric oven.

One Christmas her cooker developed a fault and so her son, by way of a Christmas present, bought her a brand new microwave oven. On the day of the next cat show, not understanding the basic difference in the technology between an ordinary electric cooker and a microwave oven, the old lady industriously washed her prize-winning Persian cat and popped it into the oven for a few seconds. There really was no miaow, nor any noise at all from the cat, for the poor creature exploded the instant the oven was switched on.

2 **elderly lady:** ältere Dame.
2 f. **pedigree cat:** Rassekatze mit Stammbaum.
4 **Persian cat:** Perserkatze (Rassekatze).
5 **to groom:** kämmen, striegeln.
15 **industriously** (adv.): fleißig.
15 f. **prize-winning:** preisgekrönt.
16 **to pop** (infml.): (hinein)schieben, -stecken.
17 **miaow:** Miauen.

Food and Drink

The Mrs. Fields Cookie Recipe

A woman supposedly calls the Mrs. Fields company headquarters in Park City, Utah, and asks for the recipe. She is told that it will be sent for a charge of "two-fifty", which she tells them to put on her credit card. When the recipe and the bill arrive, the charge is $250 – not $2.50, as she expected. For revenge, the outraged woman duplicates the recipe and sends it out to all her friends and relatives.
That woman, if she exists, must have thousands of acquaintances and a very large family, since photocopied sheets telling some version of this story have shown up everywhere, with the recipe appended. The Mrs. Fields telephone lines were kept busy with queries about it.

2 **Mrs. Fields:** Kette, die frische Cookies verkauft (meist in kleinen Geschäften in Einkaufszentren).
3 **supposedly** (adv.): angeblich.
6 **to put s.th. on s.o.'s credit card:** jds. Kreditkarte mit etwas belasten.
8 **outraged:** empört.
9 **to duplicate:** vervielfältigen.
14 **to append:** anhängen, -fügen.
15 **query:** Nach-, Anfrage.

Squeaky Canned Cola

Two friends stopped at a roadside café to have a snack. As it was a warm sunny day, they ordered sandwiches and cans of cola intending to sit outside and have lunch. As they drank, one of the friends commented that his cola tasted a little strange. However, he thought no more of it until he came to pour the last glassful out of the can. Much to his surprise the body of a half-decomposed mouse dropped into his glass. The poor man was taken to hospital and, fortunately, he was found to be unharmed. Allegedly, he sued the cola manufacturers and received several thousand pounds in damages.

1 **squeaky:** quietschend.
canned: in der Dose, Dosen-. Testdosen mit Kronkorkenverschluß, die aussahen wie Bierflaschen und eine größere Öffnung (durch die eine Maus hindurch passen würde) hatten, gab es schon in den frühen vierziger Jahren – die Dose, die wir kennen, kam erst 1963 auf den Markt (vgl. Thomas Jeier / Hans-Georg Fischer, *Das Coca-Cola Kultbuch*, München: Heyne, 1986, S. 94–97).
2 **roadside café:** Raststätte.
6 f. **he thought no more of it:** er machte sich keine Gedanken darüber.
9 **half-decomposed:** halbverwest.
11 **unharmed:** unversehrt.
allegedly (adv.): angeblich.

Notes

Particularly widespread in North America, this is one legend which may have some basis in fact rather than supposition. Since at least 1914, there have been several actions in the United States against local cola franchises by individuals who have found foreign bodies, including mice, in cola drinks. Whilst the legends themselves are not necessarily based on these isolated instances, such legal actions do provide a climate which reinforces existing legends.
In addition to the above tale, many other stories and beliefs circulate amongst children. Predominant among these is the belief that if meat is left to soak in cola overnight it will dissolve.

3 **supposition:** Annahme, Vermutung.
8 **to reinforce:** (fig.) verstärken, untermauern.
9 **to circulate:** im Umlauf sein.
10 **to be predominant:** vorherrschend sein, an erster Stelle stehen.
11 **to soak:** eingeweicht werden.

[Illustration] **grotty:** mies, scheußlich.

The Perfect Mousse

A young housewife was to give her first dinner party and her husband had invited several directors from his firm. As it was to be a special dinner, one of the things she intended to prepare was a salmon mousse. With this in mind, she went to the local market, purchased the necessary fish and, after cleaning it, left it on the kitchen table while she gathered up the rest of the ingredients. Returning from the larder, to her horror, she found the cat sitting on the table chewing the fish. She chased the cat away and thought – "Well, it is not as if they will know that the cat has nibbled the fish." Accordingly she washed and cleaned it again and got on with her preparations.

The dinner party was a great success and, as the evening came to a close, the guests went off into the night making many complimentary comments, particularly about the salmon mousse. Closing the gates after the last car had left, the couple suddenly noticed, by the side of the house porch, their cat very stiff and very dead.

1 **mousse:** Mousse (Schaumspeise).
5 **salmon:** Lachs.
9 **larder:** Vorratsschrank, Speisekammer.
10 **to chew:** hier: anknabbern.
11 **to chase away:** fortjagen.
12 **to nibble:** anknabbern.
13 f. **to get on with s.th.:** mit etwas weitermachen.
16 **to come to a close:** dem Ende zugehen.
17 **complimentary:** anerkennend, schmeichelhaft.
20 **porch:** Veranda (AE).

Racking her brains, the young housewife tried to think what could have happened to the poor animal, when she remembered the salmon. Thinking the fish must have been contaminated, in desperation she grabbed the phone and called all the dinner guests, including her husband's directors, to explain and advise them to contact their doctors immediately. They were not amused and, in fact, several of the guests were very upset even to think that she had given them food the cat had chewed.

Just as she had made the last call the door-bell rang and there stood their next-door neighbour looking very sheepish. He explained that earlier in the evening he had unfortunately run over their cat in his drive. He was very sorry but he had been in a desperate hurry at the time as he was on his way to meet a train. He had rung the door-bell several times in order to tell them of the accident but, unfortunately, he could not make anyone hear above the noise of the dinner party. Instead, he had left the cat by the porch – had they found it yet?

4 **contaminated:** mit Krankheitskeimen verseucht.
in desperation: verzweifelt.
13 **sheepish:** kleinlaut, verlegen.

The Kentucky Fried Rat

Two couples stopped one night at a notable carry-out for a fried chicken snack. The husband returned to the car with the chicken. While sitting there in the car eating their chicken, his wife said, "My chicken tastes funny." She continued to eat and continued to complain.

After a while the husband said, "Let me see it." The driver of the car decided to cut the light on and then it was discovered that the woman was eating a rodent, nicely floured and fried crisp. The woman went into shock and was rushed to the hospital. It was reported that the husband was approached by lawyers representing the carry-out and offered the sum of $35,000. The woman remained on the critical list for several days. Spokesmen from the hospital would not divulge the facts about the case and nurses were instructed to keep

1 **Kentucky Fried Rat:** Wortspiel mit *Kentucky Fried Chicken* (amerikanische Schnellrestaurantkette, in der v. a. Brathähnchen serviert werden).
2 **notable:** bekannt.
carry-out: Schnellrestaurant, in dem man Speisen zum Mitnehmen bekommt.
9 **to cut the light on:** das Licht einschalten.
10 **rodent:** Nagetier.
11 **floured:** paniert.
crisp: knusprig.
15 **to remain on the critical list:** sich weiterhin in einem kritischen Zustand befinden.
16 **spokesman:** Sprecher.
to divulge: preisgeben.

their mouths shut. And it is also reported that a second offer was made for $75,000, and this too was refused. The woman died and presumably the case will come to court.

3 f. **to come to court:** vor Gericht kommen.

A Mix-up in the Mail

Grandmother had gone out to spend Christmas with her cousins who lived in the Far East. She had not seen them for several years and was very excited about the trip. They had always been very kind to her and each Christmas they used to send a present of a jar of special spices to go in the Christmas cake her daughter made.

About two weeks before Christmas, a small airmail parcel arrived from the Far East. It had been posted on 1 December and contained what appeared to be the special spices for the Christmas cake. There was no note with it nor, surprisingly, any Christmas card. Not wanting to delay any longer, the daughter got on with the baking and produced a magnificent cake for the Christmas festivities.

It was the day after Boxing Day that a letter arrived from the cousins in the Far East. Also dated 1 December, it expressed how sorry they were to have to break the news of grandmother's death – the excitement had been too much for her. They also wrote that, because of all the arrangements that had had to be made for the cremation, they would not have time to send over the

1 **mix-up:** Verwechslung.
3 **Far East:** ferner Osten.
6 **jar:** (Schraub-)Glas.
7 **spices:** Gewürze.
to go in the cake: als Zutaten für den Kuchen.
17 **Boxing Day:** zweiter Weihnachtsfeiertag.
23 **cremation:** Einäscherung.

special spices for the cake this year. However, they had airmailed grandmother's ashes home and they should arrive shortly.

Notes

This charming story of family life has circulated, both in the form of a joke and a legend, for many years. Certainly it was known in Michigan, USA, back in 1955 and, more recently, provided the plot for a one-act play by Pat Wilson, *Funeral Tea* (1972).

5 **to circulate:** im Umlauf sein.

At Work

Tragedy in the Bakery

Working on the early shift a baker, perhaps not quite as awake as he should have been, fell into the dough machine. The machine was quickly turned off but sadly the baker had been killed and his body all chewed up and mixed in with the dough.
His wife was notified, of course, as was the coroner and eventually, after the post-mortem, the bakery was told they could clean out the dough machine and put it back into service. The machine was duly cleaned out and production restarted. Unfortunately, the job was not done thoroughly and a few weeks later the poor baker's widow, who had been granted free bread for her life from the company, was slicing up a loaf when she found her husband's signet ring inside.

3 **early shift:** Frühschicht.
4 f. **dough machine:** Knetmaschine für Teig.
6 **to chew up:** hier: zerstückeln.
8 **to notify:** benachrichtigen.
coroner: Beamter, der gewaltsame oder unnatürliche Todesfälle untersucht; etwa: Gerichtsmediziner.
9 **post-mortem:** Obduktion.
14 **free:** kostenlos.
16 **signet ring:** Siegelring.

[Illustration] **done:** durch, gar.
parsley: Petersilie.
sage: Salbei.

Dangers of the Microwave Oven I

In the kitchens of a large hotel a microwave oven had been installed. However, rather than being set at eye level, like the majority of such ovens, this one was fitted down low – almost at waist height in fact. One day a young pastry chef, who worked at a table across the aisle from this cooker, was suddenly taken ill and in seconds collapsed and died.

On investigation it was discovered that every time he stepped back to admire his handywork he stood with his back against the microwave oven door. Unfortunately, the oven door did not seal properly and over a period of time it had slowly cooked his kidneys and it was this that had eventually killed him.

3 f. **at eye level:** in, auf Augenhöhe.
6 **pastry chef:** Konditor.
7 **aisle:** Gang.
10 **handywork:** Arbeit, Werk.
12 **to seal:** hier: fest schließen.
13 **kidney:** Niere.

The Minced Butcher

It is only in a few butchers' shops that sausages are still made by hand on the premises, and recently I heard of one butcher who still continued this practice. Every Wednesday afternoon he worked in the back room of his shop preparing sausages for the following week. He had a large grinding machine and into it he pushed the ingredients which were minced up and slowly fed into the sausage skins.

Well, this particular day, the butcher was pushing the meat in with his hand and as he worked he thought, "This is lasting a long time." As he reached over to add further ingredients he nearly fainted, for he suddenly realized that his hand had gone. He had minced his hand clean away and had never felt a thing.

1 **to mince:** kleinhacken (vgl. *minced meat:* Hackfleisch).
3 **on the premises** (pl.): vor Ort.
7 **grinding machine:** Fleischwolf.
9 **sausage skin:** Wursthaut.
15 **clean away** (adv.): glatt weg.

The Ice-Cream-Cone Caper

The Great Ice-Cream-Cone-Caper of 1986 was an embarrassing example of news reporting gone awry when confronted with an emerging urban legend. In case you stayed home that summer with the plug pulled on your TV and all the papers canceled, here's how the cone caper went. Either Paul Newman in Wesport, Connecticut (or Jack Nicholson in Cohasset, Massachusetts, or Robert Redford in Santa Fe, New Mexico, or even Tom Brokaw somewhere else), is in a local ice-cream store. A woman comes in and recognizes the star. She is on the verge of swooning with ecstasy, but she is determined to remain calm and not disgrace herself or invade the star's privacy. So she buys a cone and departs without saying anything, but outside the store she realizes that, while she has her change,

1 **ice-cream cone:** Eiswaffel, -tüte.
caper: ‚Geschichte', ‚Sache'. Diese Geschichte wurde 1995 vom *Stern* wiederbelebt, in der Version mit Paul Newman.
3 **to go awry:** in die Irre gehen.
6 **to cancel:** (Zeitung) abbestellen.
7 **Newman:** Paul N. (geb. 1925), amerikanischer Filmschauspieler.
8 **Nicholson:** Jack N. (geb. 1937), amerikanischer Filmschauspieler.
9 **Redford:** Robert R. (geb. 1937), amerikanischer Filmschauspieler.
10 **Brokaw:** Tom B. (geb. 1940), populärer amerikanischer Reporter und Nachrichtenredakteur, zuletzt bei NBC.
12 **to be on the verge of doing s.th.:** kurz davor, drauf und dran sein, etwas zu tun.
12 f. **to swoon with ecstasy:** vor Entzücken vergehen, schier ohnmächtig werden.
13 f. **to disgrace o.s.:** sich zum Idioten machen, blamieren.
14 **to invade s.o.'s privacy:** jds. Privatsphäre verletzen.

she's missing her ice-cream cone. She goes back in to claim what is rightly hers, whereupon the celebrity – licking his own cone – comments, "You'll find it in your purse, ma'am – right where you put it."

2 **celebrity:** Berühmtheit, Star.
3 **to lick:** lecken, schlecken.
4 **purse:** Handtasche (AE).

The Grocery Scam

A young man is shopping in a supermarket, when he notices that an older woman seems to be following him, staring at him in a sorrowful manner. He moves to the next aisle, trying to avoid her, but she follows, still staring.

And when he finishes shopping, he ends up behind her in a long checkout line. Her grocery basket is full to overflowing; his contains just a few items.

She keeps staring at him, sadly, making him feel most uncomfortable.

Finally, she speaks up. "You must pardon my staring," she says, "but you see, you look exactly like my son who died just two weeks ago."

And she begins to sniffle as she repeats her claim that the young man perfectly resembles her late, beloved son. "I mean *exactly* like him," she moans.

Then, as the cashier bags her groceries at the front of the line, the woman whispers, "As a favor to a grief-stricken mother, would you mind saying 'Good-by, Mom' to me as I leave? Somehow it would make me feel so much better."

1 **scam** (AE, slang): Masche.
4 **sorrowful:** traurig, betrübt.
5 **aisle:** Gang.
8 **checkout:** Kasse.
8 f. **full to overflowing:** übervoll.
11 **uncomfortable:** unbehaglich.
15 **to sniffle:** schniefen.
18 **cashier:** Kassiererin.
19 f. **grief-stricken:** gramgebeugt.

The young man gulps and agrees to her pathetic request. She gives him a tearful smile, waves, and wheels out her three heavy bags.

"Good-by, Mom," he says, waving back.

All the scene needs to make it perfect melodrama is violins welling up in the background or maybe a little supermarket Muzak. But before your heart strings are tugged too tightly, listen to how the legend ends:

The young man, reflecting on his good deed, feels such a warm glow of self-satisfaction that he barely notices the cashier ringing up his own purchases. Until, that is, the cashier tells him that the bill comes to $110.

"There must be a mistake," the young man says, pointing at his single small bag.

"Your mother said you'd be paying for hers, too," the cashier says.

1 **to gulp:** schlucken.
pathetic: herzergreifend.
2 **a tearful smile:** ein Lächeln unter Tränen.
6 **to well up:** erklingen, einsetzen.
7 **Muzak:** Gebrauchsmusik (wie sie auf Supermarkt-Tonbändern läuft).
7 f. **to tug at s.o.'s heart strings:** jdm. das Herz zerreißen.
10 **glow** (fig.): Glücksgefühl.
self-satisfaction: Selbstzufriedenheit.
11 **to ring up:** eintippen, zusammenrechnen.

The Will

A woman is shopping on Madison Avenue in New York City, when she needs to use a restroom. Finding none in any of the stores, she enters a funeral home – the only other public place nearby – and uses the restroom there.

On the way out, she passes a darkened room decorated with flowers. In the center of the room is an open coffin with a dead man's (or woman's) body inside. There are no visitors in sight.

She feels a little guilty about using the facilities on the sly, so she steps into the room and signs the guest book.

Not long afterward she gets a call from the dead man's (or woman's) lawyer (or the state attorney general), who says that the deceased, a person of great wealth, had provided $10,000 in his (or her) will to whoever attended his funeral. The woman had been the only person to show up.

3 **restroom:** Toilette.
4 **funeral home** (AE): Bestattungsunternehmen.
7 **darkened:** abgedunkelt.
11 f. **on the sly:** heimlich.
12 f. **guest book:** hier: Kondolenzbuch.
16 **to decease:** versterben.

Ornithology

There is another story that also involves a student who is unknown to the professor. This student was taking an ornithology class, for which the final exam counted as half the grade. When the professor handed him his exam, the student was shocked to find that the entire exam was just pictures of birds' legs, with the directions "Identify each species." (In a variation, the professor sets up a row of stuffed birds with bags over their bodies so that only their feet show.) The student was furious and stormed up to the front of the class, ripped his paper into little pieces, handed them to the professor, and said, "This is ridiculous!"

The professor shouted back, "You can't do that!"

And the student returned, "I sure as hell can!"

The professor then screamed, "Then you're going to fail this class. What's your name, anyway?" And he pulled out his grade book to note down the offender's fate.

The student then pulled up his right pants leg to the knee and said, "You tell me, Prof."

1 **ornithology:** Ornithologie, Vogelkunde.
5 **grade:** Note, Zensur.
8 **species:** Spezies, Art.
10 f. **furious:** wütend.
11 **to rip:** (zer)reißen.
15 **sure as hell:** aber sicher, todsicher.
18 **grade book:** Zensurenbuch.
offender: Täter.

Trouble with Technology

I've heard several times from bank personnel about a frustrated robber who they believe tried to hold up an automatic teller machine somewhere. (It was never the storyteller's own bank.) The man allegedly wrote a note saying "Give me all your money, or I'll shoot" and inserted the slip of paper into the bank's ATM. When three such attempts gained him nothing, the man is said to have become so angry that he shot the machine full of holes, thus attracting the police, who arrested him.

3 **frustrated:** frustriert.
4 **automatic teller machine:** Geldautomat.
5 **allegedly** (adv.): angeblich.
7 **to insert:** (ein)schieben.
ATM: Kurzform von *automatic teller machine.*

The Everlasting Light Bulb

It was around 1920, shortly after he had married, when the old man originally purchased the light bulb from a small store in town. It appeared to be a normal light bulb. However, when after sixty years it was still going strong, he decided to write to the manufacturers and tell them of this remarkable phenomenon.

By return a reply came from the company indicating they were very interested in the bulb and would like to send someone to see it. Eventually, one of the directors of the firm called and, instead of just showing interest, offered to buy it for £1,000.

The old man, of course, refused, as the light bulb had given him good service. However, his curiosity was certainly aroused – why so much money for his light bulb? The director could provide no plausible explanation as to why they were willing to offer so much for the bulb, so the old man decided to explore this mystery further.

With the help of a solicitor friend he did a little investigating and discovered that in the 1920s this particular light-bulb manufacturer had bought and tested the patent for an everlasting light bulb. Only a few of these bulbs were made and the company, finding the invention worked, destroyed the bulbs and suppressed the

1 **everlasting light bulb:** Glühbirne, die nie kaputtgeht.
5 f. **to be going strong:** gut funktionieren.
14 **to give s.o. good service:** jdm. gute Dienste leisten.
20 **solicitor friend:** befreundeter Rechtsanwalt.

idea – after all, it would have put them out of business. Unknown to the company one of the lights had accidentally become mixed up with a batch of ordinary bulbs and this was the light bulb which had lit the old man's kitchen for the past sixty years.

Notes

Stories of suppressed enterprise, of one sort or another, have regularly emerged since the end of the Second World War. In addition to everlasting light bulbs, wonder drugs and carburettors or spark plugs that would give drivers 100 miles to the gallon have also featured in such legends.

It is interesting to observe that since the western world has become somewhat more energy-conscious, the number of low-power, long-life bulbs on the market has increased and so reversed the attitudes expressed in this narrative.

1 **to put s.o. out of business:** jdn. arbeitslos machen.
3 **batch:** hier: Charge.
9 **carburettor:** Vergaser.
spark plug: Zündkerze.
10 **100 miles to the gallon:** etwa: 2,5 l auf 100 km.
12 f. **to become energy-conscious:** bewußt mit Energie umgehen, Strom sparen.
13 **low-power:** energiesparend.

[Illustration] **Honesty is the best policy** (prov.): Ehrlich währt am längsten.

my policy is first party only: etwa: ich bin mir selbst der Nächste.

Cars

No Claim

Returning to the car he had left in a nearby car park, a friend of a cousin of mine was rather perturbed to find one side of the vehicle all scratched and dinted. Seeing a note on the windscreen, he breathed a sigh of relief, for he thought that the culprit had left his name and address so, at least, he could make a claim for the damage against the other driver's insurance company. However, on opening the note, his relief turned to dismay when he read:

> Dear Driver,
> I have just run into your car and made a hell of a mess of it. As a crowd has gathered, I am forced to appear as if writing you this note to apologize and to leave you my name and address. As you can see, however, this I have not done.
> A Well-Wisher

4 **perturbed:** verstört.
5 **dinted:** verbeult, eingedellt.
6 **to breathe a sigh of relief:** einen Seufzer der Erleichterung ausstoßen.
7 **culprit:** Schuldiger.
10 **dismay:** Bestürzung.
12f. **to make a hell of a mess of s.th.:** etwas total ruinieren.
17 **well-wisher:** Sympathisant(in); jd., der alles Gute wünscht.

The Death Car

One evening some years ago a friend of mine found an advertisement in the newspaper for a secondhand car. It had only one previous owner and the price was unbelievable – less than half my friend would normally have expected to pay. He immediately drove round to see the car and, finding it was still for sale, he gave it a thorough examination – after all, at that price there must be something wrong with it! Well, after giving it a good going-over, he could not find anything wrong with it except the interior had a rather peculiar smell and it had a blood stain on the front seat. In spite of this, my friend decided the car was an excellent buy, so he paid up and it was delivered the following day.
Over the next week, however, the smell in the car persisted. No matter how much he cleaned the upholstery he could not remove the stain and, if anything, the smell seemed to be getting worse. Finally, in desperation, he returned the car to the showroom. To his astonishment they offered to refund his money without question. Thinking this was strange, he asked the manager what caused the smell. The manager explained that the previous owner had committed sui-

4 **previous owner:** Vorbesitzer.
10 **going-over:** Überprüfung.
16 **to persist:** bleiben, anhalten.
16 f. **upholstery:** Polster.
18 f. **in desperation:** verzweifelt.
19 **showroom:** Verkaufsraum.
20 **to refund:** zurückzahlen.

cide in the car while it was parked in the garage at home. Unfortunately, the body had not been found for several weeks.

Notes

Frequently reported in both the British Isles and North America since 1950, this story has been traced back, by the American folklorist Richard Dorson, to an alleged incident in Mecosta, Michigan, USA in 1938. The widespread circulation of this legend, and the fact that many alternative towns and types of car are reported, tends to indicate that the Mecosta incident possibly did not start the story but rather acted to reinforce an older tale.

7 **alleged:** angeblich.
11 **to reinforce:** untermauern.

The Unstealable Car

A man has this classic sports car that he labored for years to restore to mint condition. He keeps it parked in his garage with the wheels on cardboard sheets, taking it out only on special occasions and in perfect weather.

Fearful of thieves, he devises a foolproof way to secure his treasure. He has thick steel staples sunk into the concrete of the garage floor, and he attaches the car using heavy chains passed through the staples and around the car's frame and secured with several locks. The car is thus parked and locked, facing into the garage, and covered with a tarp.

The next time he removes the tarp preparing to drive his sports car, he finds the vehicle still solidly chained down and locked – but now facing outward. Under a wiper blade is this note: "If we want this car, we'll take it."

3 **mint condition:** tadelloser Zustand.
4 **cardboard sheet:** Pappe.
8 **staple:** Krampe.
12 f. **facing into the garage:** vorwärts in die Garage (geparkt).
13 **tarp:** Kurzform von *tarpaulin:* Plane.
17 **wiper blade:** Scheibenwischer, Wischblatt.

On the Road and in the Air

The Unlucky Escape

To celebrate buying a brand new white Rover car, my friend thought he would go out for a night with the boys.
As he drove home along the motorway in the fog after consuming several pints of beer, a police car drew in alongside and forced him to pull over. The policeman asked my friend to step out of his car and was just about to tell him to "blow into this, please", when close by there was a loud crash, followed by another and another – a multiple pile-up had started.
Ordering my friend not to go away, the policeman ran off in the direction of the noise. After a split second's deliberation my friend was in the car and on his way home. When he arrived he locked the car in the garage and told his wife, if anyone enquired where he was, to say he had been ill in bed for the last twenty-four hours.

4 f. **with the boys** (infml.): mit seinen Freunden, mit seiner Männerclique.
7 f. **to draw in alongside:** seitlich heranfahren.
12 **multiple pile-up:** Massenkarambolage.
14 **split second:** Sekundenbruchteil.
15 **deliberation:** Überlegung, Nachdenken.

It was later the following morning when the police called and asked to see her husband. "I'm sorry," the wife informed them, "but my husband is ill in bed with 'flu." "Could we possibly have a look at his car?" the police asked. "Certainly," she replied. However, when she opened the garage doors, she was somewhat amazed to see, not her husband's white Rover, but a Rover with red and blue stripes down the sides and a blue flashing light on the roof.

Note

This well-reported story has been circulating in the British Isles since the early 1970s.

9 **blue flashing light:** Blaulicht.

[Illustration] **to nick** (slang): klauen.

The Vanishing Hitchhiker

Well, this happened to one of my girlfriend's best friends and her father. They were driving along a country road on their way home from the cottage when they saw a young girl hitchhiking. They stopped and picked her up and she got in the back seat. She told the girl and her father that she just lived in the house about five miles up the road. She didn't say anything after that, but just turned to watch out the window. When the father saw the house, he drove up to it and turned around to tell the girl they had arrived – but she wasn't there! Both he and his daughter were really mystified and decided to knock on the door and tell the people what had happened. They told them that they had once had a daughter who answered the description of the girl they supposedly had picked up, but she had disappeared some years ago and had last been seen hitchhiking on this very road. Today would have been her birthday.

1 **hitchhiker:** Tramper(in).
12 **to be mystified:** vor einem Rätsel stehen.

The Two Hitchhikers

In the Seattle version, a traveling salesman is driving alone on a long haul between Seattle and Spokane and decides to pick up a hitchhiker to keep him company. But the rider immediately makes him uneasy. The man is middle-aged, scruffy, poorly dressed, and keeps turning around in the front seat as if looking for something to steal.

The driver decides to stop for a second hitchhiker, this time for security. He picks one who is young, clean-cut, well dressed, and who looks thoroughly respectable. This young man gets into the back seat.

Appearances are deceptive, however. As soon as the car with the three occupants is underway again, the young man in back pulls out a gun, points it at the driver, and orders him to stop. As the car slows to a halt, he gestures with the gun for the two to get out.

The moment the gun is moved off its target, however, the older hitchhiker in the front seat takes advantage of the situation, jumps at the would-be mugger, and, with a quick, powerful blow, knocks him cold. Then, to the driver's astonishment, he extracts the young man's wal-

2 **traveling salesman:** Handelsvertreter.
6 **scruffy:** heruntergekommen.
10 **clean-cut:** sauber, anständig.
13 **appearances are deceptive** (pl.): der Schein trügt.
14 **occupant:** Insasse.
to be underway: in Bewegung sein, weiterfahren.
20 **would-be:** Möchtegern-.
21 **to knock s.o. cold:** jdn. k.o. schlagen.

let and offers to split evenly with the driver the two twenty dollar bills he finds there.

"He's new in the business," the hitchhiker says. "He'll have to learn that a gun ain't a pointer. I've been in the business twenty years, and I don't make dumb mistakes anymore."

The driver is aghast. He numbly refuses the money, and he looks frightened enough so that his rescuer finally understands his thoughts.

"Oh, I ain't working today," the man says. "I'm just going to Spokane on a visit."

1 **to split evenly:** halbe-halbe machen.
4 **ain't** (slang): *is not.*
pointer: Zeigestab.
7 **aghast:** erschreckt.
numbly (adv.): wie betäubt, abwesend.
10 **ain't** (slang): *am not.*

[Illustration] **L:** Abk. für *Learner* (Plakette, die in Großbritannien aufs Auto geklebt wird, wenn man noch keine Fahrpraxis hat).

The Auto-Pilot

The flight ran several times a week taking holiday-makers to various resorts in the Mediterranean. On each flight, to reassure the passengers all was well, the captain would put the jet on to auto-pilot and he and all the crew would come aft into the cabin to greet the passengers.
Unfortunately, on this particular flight the security door between the cabin and the flight deck jammed and left the captain and crew stuck in the cabin. From that moment, in spite of the efforts to open the door, the fate of the passengers and crew was sealed.

3 **Mediterranean:** Mittelmeer.
4 **to reassure:** beruhigen.
6 **aft** (adv., aeronaut.): achtern, nach hinten.
9 **flight deck:** Cockpit.
11 **in spite of:** trotz.
12 **to seal:** besiegeln.

The Ghost Airliner

There was this father and daughter who both worked for Eastern. He was a pilot – captain or something, I think – and she was a stewardess. He was flying a DC-8 or DC-10 or something, I can't remember, but he crashed the plane and was killed. Well, his daughter kept on flying and on one trip (on the same kind of aircraft her father was killed on) her father's ghost appeared to her and told her the wiring in the plane was faulty, and sure enough, when they checked there was a fire in the wiring. They say that he appeared to her when she opened the door of a warmer oven – his face was there. He appeared to other people on that same kind of aircraft and told them that that kind of plane was unsafe.

3 **Eastern:** *Eastern Airways:* Luftfahrtgesellschaft.
9 **wiring:** Kabel, elektrische Leitung.
10 **faulty:** fehlerhaft, defekt.
12 **warmer oven:** Ofen, in dem an Bord die Speisen aufgewärmt werden.

The Second Death

The class toured a mortuary, and an employee there told a story that "one of our drivers heard had happened to a friend of his in the same kind of job."

The mortuary employee was sent out in a hearse to pick up the body of an elderly woman who had died in the night. While the employee was returning to the mortuary, he heard a gurgling noise in the back of the hearse.

At first, he thought it was merely the sound of an air bubble escaping from the corpse, which had been jostled about when the hearse drove over potholes in the road. But when the noise continued, the employee stopped the vehicle and went around to the back to check. He unzipped the body bag and found that the "corpse" was actually still alive. The bumpy ride had aroused the woman from a coma.

The employee immediately called a nearby hospital, relayed his location, and was instructed to drive toward

2 **class:** gemeint sind Studierende, die sich im Rahmen ihres Studiums mit Sterberitualen befassen.
mortuary: Leichenschauhaus.
5 **hearse:** Leichenwagen.
6 **elderly woman:** ältere Dame.
8 **to gurgle:** gluckern, glucksen.
11 f. **to jostle about:** herumstoßen.
12 **pothole:** Schlagloch.
15 **to unzip s.th.:** den Reißverschluß von etwas öffnen.
body bag: Kunststoffsack für Todesopfer.
16 **bumpy:** holperig.
18 f. **to relay:** durchgeben, mitteilen.

the hospital. An ambulance would meet him en route, and the woman would be transferred to it for emergency treatment.

But in his excitement, the employee drove too fast, and the hearse collided with a vehicle in the other lane – the oncoming ambulance. In a twist worthy of O. Henry, the woman in the back of the hearse was killed.

1 **en route:** unterwegs.
2 f. **emergency treatment:** Notfalltherapie.
5 **to collide:** zusammenstoßen.
6 **twist** (fig.): (überraschende) Wendung.
7 **O. Henry:** d. i. William Sidney Porter (1862–1910), amerikanischer Kurzgeschichtenautor, für dessen Stil überraschende Schlußpointen charakteristisch sind.

Holidays and Leisure

The Disappearing Room

Two spinster ladies, on a travelling holiday in France, arrived at their hotel rather late one night. They were placed in adjoining rooms and, as they were weary, both fell into a heavy sleep. Awaking in the late morning one of the ladies went into the next room to see her friend. She was perplexed to find it was not the room that she had seen the night before – the wallpaper and furnishings were all quite different and, more to the point, her friend was not there.
When she asked the receptionist where her companion was the reply came, "What companion, madame? You arrived alone." Rather confused the lady asked other members of the hotel staff the same question but always received the same reply, "Madame, you arrived alone."
Quite determined to get to the bottom of the matter,

3 **spinster lady:** altes Fräulein.
5 **adjoining:** nebeneinanderliegend, angrenzend.
6 **heavy sleep:** tiefer Schlaf.
8 **perplexed:** vollkommen verwirrt.
10 **furnishings** (pl.): Möbel, Einrichtung.
10 f. **more to the point:** was noch wesentlicher war.
18 **to get to the bottom of the matter:** der Sache auf den Grund gehen.

she finally went to the British Consulate who, in turn, called the police. The police reluctantly investigated what, to them, seemed a very strange story. However, much to their surprise the truth finally did come out. It transpired that the companion, shortly after retiring to bed, was taken violently ill and died. When the doctor arrived he diagnosed the cause of death as cholera. Shocked, the manager of the hotel had bribed the doctor to keep silent and an attempt to conceal the visit of the companion was planned. The body was removed, all the furnishings and fittings were destroyed and replaced. Similarly, the staff were told never to admit that anything had ever happened. Unfortunately they did not take into account the tenacity of the dead lady's friend.

5 **to transpire:** (fig.) herauskommen.
5 f. **to retire to bed:** schlafen gehen.
8 **to bribe:** bestechen.
9 **to conceal:** verdecken, verheimlichen.
11 **fittings** (pl.): (Zimmer-)Ausstattung.
14 **tenacity:** Hartnäckigkeit, Beharrlichkeit.

Notes

Alexander Woollcott in *While Rome Burns* (1934) traced this tale to an account in the *Detroit Free Press* in 1889 before the trail went cold. In 1938 the director, Veit Harlan, set the story in the Paris Exposition of 1868 and created the film *Verwehte Spuren* ("Like Sand in the Wind"). This film was subsequently remade as *So Long at the Fair* (1950). More recently the idea has been used in an episode of *Hart to Hart* on British television.

3 **before the trail went cold:** wo sich die Spur verlor.
6 **to remake:** neu verfilmen, in neuer Besetzung drehen.

[Illustration] **la plage** (Fr.): Strand; Wortspiel mit *plague* ›Pest‹.

The Nude in the RV

It was really quite simple, an American tourist explained to Royal Canadian Mounted Police who found him wandering along a highway near here clad in his undershorts. His story:
His wife was driving the family car, while he relaxed in a trailer. She stopped to let some bears cross the road and the husband stepped out to see what the trouble was.
His wife drove on.
The police drove 70 miles before overhauling the wife and reuniting the couple.

1 **nude:** Nackter.
RV (AE): Kurzform von *recreational vehicle:* Wohnmobil.
3 **Royal Canadian Mounted Police:** kanadische berittene Polizei.
4 **clad in:** bekleidet mit.
5 **undershorts** (pl.): Unterhose.
7 **trailer:** Wohnwagenanhänger.
11 **to overhaul** (CE): überholen.

The Dead Scuba Diver

The story was told to me by a friend of mine, who heard it from a friend of his. His friend is a scuba diver and said the story is "popular lore among divers."

It is the day after a forest fire, and a ranger is examining the fire and water damage caused by the blaze when he notices a human body tangled in the branches of a blackened tree. A rescue team retrieves the corpse and shows it to the ranger, who is shocked by what he sees. It is the body of a scuba diver wearing a wet suit, a mask, flippers, and an oxygen tank.

Yes, a scuba diver found dead in a tree. Incredible.

The puzzled ranger finally comes up with an explanation. To put out the fire, firefighting planes scooped water from a nearby lake and then dumped it on the blaze. The diver, the ranger figured, accidentally became part of the plane's cargo.

1 **scuba diver:** Gerätetaucher.
4 **lore:** Überlieferung, Folklore.
5 **forest fire:** Waldbrand.
ranger: Forstaufseher.
6 **blaze:** Feuer.
7 **tangled:** verheddert.
8 **blackened:** hier: rußgeschwärzt.
to retrieve: bergen.
10 **wet suit:** Taucheranzug.
11 **mask:** Tauchermaske.
flippers: Schwimmflossen.
14 **firefighting plane:** Löschflugzeug.
to scoop: schöpfen.
15 **to dump:** abwerfen, kippen.

The Vanishing Grandmother

During a camping holiday in Spain grandmother, who had been brought along with the rest of the family, died during the night of natural causes. Not wanting to bury her in a foreign country, where they might never be able to visit her grave again, the family decided to head for home and attempt to smuggle her through Spain and France and so back to England. With this in mind, they rolled grandmother's body in a carpet, tied it on to the roof rack of the car, along with the camping equipment, and started on their journey.

They drove all night and, just before breakfast, they heaved a sigh of relief as they crossed the border out of Spain and into France.

By this time all the family were very tired and hungry. As a stop for breakfast sounded a good idea, they parked the car in a side street next to a suitable café. Not wanting to leave the corpse for too long and also wishing to continue their journey as soon as possible, they ate a hasty breakfast and returned to the car. However, to their horror, their possessions had been stolen from the roof of the car including the carpet and grandmother's corpse. The funny thing is the body never did turn up.

3f. **to die of natural causes:** eines natürlichen Todes sterben.
7 **to smuggle:** schmuggeln.
10 **roof rack:** Dachgepäckträger.
13 **to heave a sigh of relief:** vor Erleichterung einen Seufzer ausstoßen.

The Fatal Tee

An army officer took a four-day leave, planning to spend all the time playing golf at the very club that adjoined the acquaintance's apartment.
From the first day, the officer got into the habit of putting the tee into his mouth after he teed off, and leaving it there as he played the course. After two days of play, he began to feel sick; and on the fourth day, he dropped dead. The course had been sprayed so heavily with pesticides that sucking on the tee had caused the officer to ingest a fatal dose of poison.

1 **tee:** Tee (kleines Plastikstäbchen mit abgeflachtem Kopf, von dem man den Golfball abschlägt).
3 f. **to adjoin s.th.:** an etwas grenzen, neben etwas liegen.
6 **to tee off:** abschlagen (Golf).
7 **to play the course:** den Platz, die Platzrunde spielen.
9 f. **pesticide:** Pestizid, Schädlingsbekämpfungsmittel.
11 **to ingest:** aufnehmen, zu sich nehmen.

Teenage Horror Stories

The Hairy-handed Hitchhiker

Driving home alone one evening a young woman notices an old lady with a large shopping bag trying to hitch a lift in her direction. Feeling charitable, and in spite of her vow never to pick up hitchhikers when alone, the girl stops and offers the hitchhiker a ride. With much gratitude the old lady accepts and gets into the car. The young woman is about to drive away when she notices that her "female" passenger has large hairy hands and wrists.

Guessing instantly that the old lady is in fact a man, she pretends to be having trouble with the car and asks "him" to get out and check if the rear lights are working. As soon as the "old lady" is round the back of the car the young woman immediately locks the doors and drives away.

2 **hairy-handed:** mit haarigen Händen.
hitchhiker: Anhalter, Tramper.
4 f. **to hitch a lift:** trampen.
5 **charitable:** großzügig, wohltätig.
5 f. **in spite of:** trotz.
6 **vow:** hier: fester Vorsatz.
8 **gratitude:** hier: Dankesbezeugung.
12 **instantly** (adv.): sofort.
14 **rear lights:** Rücklichter.

In fear she goes straight to the police station where she is questioned and the car is searched. In the shopping bag the hairy-handed hitchhiker has left behind, the police find a large and very sharp blood-stained axe – all ready for the next victim.

Note

Versions of this comparatively well-known story have been circulating in England certainly since the early 1800s.

1 **in fear:** verängstigt.
4 **blood-stained:** blutbefleckt.
7 **comparatively** (adv.): vergleichsweise.
to circulate: im Umlauf sein.

The Hook

Like many young couples still living at home the only place for Sue and Phil to do their courting was in the back of the car Phil borrowed from his father. On these evenings they would drive out to a secluded lovers lane and have a quiet, if somewhat energetic, time. One evening they were in the car following their regular athletic pursuits when, suddenly, the music on the radio was interrupted with a newsflash – a murderer had escaped from the local mental hospital. His distinguishing feature was the absence of a hand which had been replaced with a hook and people were warned to keep clear of him as he was very dangerous.

As they were parked near the mental hospital Sue became very upset and asked Phil to take her home. He replied by saying, "Oh! don't worry I'll close all the windows and lock the doors – and besides, who would want to disturb us?" Well, Sue was not placated by this and, thinking she could hear noises around the car, she became more and more upset. Finally she broke down in tears and Phil, in spite of his previous plans, agreed to take her home.

5 **secluded:** versteckt.
lovers lane: abgelegene Gasse als beliebter Treffpunkt für Liebespaare.
8 **pursuit:** Zeitvertreib.
9 **newsflash:** Kurzmeldung.
10 f. **distinguishing feature:** besonderes Kennzeichen.
12 f. **to keep clear of s.o.:** jdm. aus dem Weg gehen.
18 **to placate s.o.:** jdn. beschwichtigen.
20 f. **to break down in tears:** in Tränen ausbrechen.
21 **in spite of:** trotz, entgegen.

As they drove home Sue started to calm down and the evening culminated with them having a farewell kiss in the car outside her parents' house. Having delayed the farewell for as long as possible Sue finally got out of the car and, turning to slam the door, screamed and collapsed in a faint. There hanging on the car door was the hook ripped from the hand of the escaped murderer.

Notes

Found in both North America and Europe, this story was well known by the mid 1950s. Often told as true amongst adolescents, it demonstrates that we have, unfortunately, indoctrinated our children with a mistrust and fear of the mentally ill and a revulsion of physical disfigurements.

2 **to culminate:** gipfeln, den Höhepunkt finden.
farewell kiss: Abschiedskuß.
5 **to slam the door:** die Tür zuwerfen, -schlagen.
5 f. **to collapse in a faint:** ohnmächtig zusammenbrechen.
7 **to rip:** (ab)reißen.
10 **adolescent:** Jugendlicher.
11 **to indoctrinate s.o. with s.th.:** jdm. etwas einflößen.
12 **mistrust:** Mißtrauen.
revulsion: Abscheu, Ekel.
12 f. **disfigurement:** Entstellung.

The Boyfriend's Death

This happened just a few years ago out on the road that turns off 59 highway by the Holiday Inn. This couple were parked under a tree out on this road. Well, it got to be time for the girl to be back at the dorm, so she told her boyfriend that they should start back. But the car wouldn't start, so he told her to lock herself in the car and he would go down to the Holiday Inn and call for help. Well, he didn't come back and he didn't come back, and pretty soon she started hearing a scratching noise on the roof of the car. "Scratch, scratch ... scratch, scratch." She got scareder and scareder, but he didn't come back. Finally, when it was almost daylight, some people came along and stopped and helped her out of the car, and she looked up and there was her boyfriend hanging from the tree, and his feet were scraping against the roof of the car. This is why the road is called "Hangman's Road."

3 **to turn off:** abbiegen.
5 **dorm:** Kurzform von *dormitory:* Studentenwohnheim (AE).
12 **scared:** verängstigt.
18 **hangman:** Erhängter.

The Baby-sitter and the Man Upstairs

Version 1

There was this baby-sitter that was in Montreal baby-sitting for three children in a big house. She was watching TV when suddenly the phone rang. The children were all in bed. She picked up the phone and heard this guy on the other end laughing hysterically. She asked him what it was that he wanted, but he wouldn't answer and then hung up. She worried about it for a while, but then thought nothing more of it and went back to watching the movie.

Everything was fine until about fifteen minutes later when the phone rang again. She picked it up and heard the same voice laughing hysterically at her, and then hung up. At this point she became really worried and phoned the operator to tell her what had been happening. The operator told her to calm down and that if he called again to try and keep him on the line as long as possible and she would try to trace the call.

Again about fifteen minutes later the guy called back and laughed hysterically at her. She asked him why he was doing this, but he just kept laughing at her. He hung up and about five seconds later the operator called. She told the girl to get out of the house at once because the person who was calling was calling from the upstairs extension. She slammed down the phone and just as she was turning to leave she saw the man

16 **operator:** Telefonvermittlung.
26 **to slam down the phone:** den Hörer auf die Gabel knallen.

coming down the stairs laughing hysterically with a bloody butcher knife in his hand and meaning to kill her. She ran out onto the street but he didn't follow. She called the police and they came and caught the man, and discovered that he had murdered all the children.

Version 2

It was August 8, 1969. She was going to baby-sit at the Smiths who had two children, ages five and seven. She had just put the children to bed and went back to the living room to watch TV.
The phone began to ring; she went to answer it; the man on the other end said, "I'm upstairs with the children; you'd better come up."
She hung the phone up immediately, scared to death. She decided that it must be a prank phone call; again she went to watch TV. The phone rang again; she went to answer it, this time more scared than last.
The man said, "I'm upstairs with the children," and described them in detail. So she hung up the phone, not knowing what to do. Should I call the police? Instead she decided, "I'll call the operator. They can trace these phone calls." She called the operator, and the operator said that she would try and do what she could. Approximately ten minutes later the phone rang again; this time she was shaking.
She answered the phone and the man again said, "I'm

16 **prank phone call:** telefonische Belästigung.

upstairs with the children; you'd better come quick!" She tried to stay on the phone as long as she could so that the operator could trace the call; this time the man hung up.

She called back, and the operator said, "Run out of the house; the man is on the extension."

She didn't quite know what to do; should she go and get the children? "No," she said, "he's up there; if I go and get the children, I'll be killed too!"

She ran next door to the neighbor's house and called the police. The sirens came – there must have been at least ten police cars. They went inside the house, ran upstairs, and found not a man, but a seven-year-old child who was sitting next to the phone with a tape recorder. Later they found that a boy down the street had told this young boy to do this next time he had a baby-sitter. You see the boy didn't like his parents going out, and he didn't like having baby-sitters. So he felt this was the only way he could get rid of them. The boys don't have baby-sitters anymore; now they go to nursery school.

11 **siren:** Sirene.

The Roommate's Death

These two girls in Corbin had stayed late over Christmas vacation. One of them had to wait for a later train, and the other wanted to go to a fraternity party given that night of vacation. The dorm assistant was in her room – sacked out. They waited and waited for the intercom, and then they heard this knocking and knocking outside in front of the dorm. So the girl thought it was her date and she went down. But she didn't come back and she didn't come back. So real late that night this other girl heard a scratching and gasping down the hall. She couldn't lock the door, so she locked herself in the closet. In the morning she let herself out and her roommate had had her throat cut, and if the other girl had opened the door earlier, she [the dead roommate] would have been saved.

1 **roommate:** Zimmergenosse, -genossin.
2 **Corbin:** *Corbin Hall:* Studentenwohnheim für Studentinnen im ersten Studienjahr an der University of Kansas.
4 **fraternity:** Studentenverbindung.
5 **dorm assistant:** Wohnheimaufsicht.
6 **to sack out** (AE, slang): einschlafen, wegknacken.
6 f. **intercom:** Gegensprechanlage.
11 **to gasp:** nach Luft schnappen, keuchen.
13 **closet:** 1. Schrank; 2. Toilette.

The Graveyard Wager

Several girls were sleeping over at one girl's home while the parents were away. After the lights were out, they started talking about the recent burial of an old man in the nearby cemetery. A rumor was going around that the man had been buried alive and had been heard trying to claw his way out.

One girl laughed at the idea, so they dared her to go out and visit the grave. As proof that she had gone, she was to drive a stake into the earth above the grave.

They sent their friend off on her errand and shut off the lights again, expecting her to return right away.

But an hour passed, and then another, without any sign of the girl. The others lay awake, gradually growing terrified. Morning came, and she still hadn't returned.

Later that day, the girl's parents arrived home, and parents and friends went together to the cemetery.

They found the girl lying on the grave – dead. When she squatted down to push the wooden stake into the ground, she drove it through the hem of her skirt.

1 **graveyard:** Friedhof.
wager (arch.): Wette.
7 **to claw one's way out:** hier: sich mit bloßen Händen zu befreien suchen.
8 **to dare:** heraus-, auffordern.
10 **stake:** Pfahl.
12 **errand:** Auftrag.
20 **to squat down:** sich hinhocken.
21 **hem:** Saum.

When she tried to stand up and couldn't, she thought the dead man had grabbed hold of her – and she died instantly of fright.

2 **to grab hold of s.o.:** jdn. festhalten.
3 **instantly** (adv.): sofort.

[Illustration] **Take a note:** Bitte schreiben Sie!, zum Diktat, bitte!
suicide note: Abschiedsbrief, bevor jd. Selbstmord begeht.

Interpersonal Relationships

Not Your Lucky Night

It was the day of the boss's birthday and his secretar quite out of the blue, invited him round to her flat aft work for a drink. She was a very good-looking woman and the boss had always been attracted to her, though neither had ever made any advance to the other. Thinking that she was for once giving him the come on, by the time they arrived at her flat, he had totally misinterpreted her intentions. So, when she gave him a large whisky and said that she must just slip into the bedroom to see to a few things, his expectations rose and, in a mad moment, he removed his clothing and stood ready and waiting for her return.

He was in fact standing just in his socks when his wife, children, friends and colleagues burst out of the bedroom carrying a large cake and singing "Happy Birthday to you . . . ."

4 **out of the blue:** ohne besonderen Anlaß, spontan.
to invite s.o. round: jdn. einladen.
5 **good-looking:** gutaussehend, attraktiv.
7 **to make advances to s.o.:** sich an jdn. heranmachen.
8 **to give s.o. the come on:** sich an jdn. heranmachen, jdm. grünes Licht geben.
9 f. **to misinterpret:** fehlinterpretieren.
11 f. **to slip into the bedroom:** kurz mal ins Schlafzimmer gehen.

[Illustration] **nightcap:** Nachtmütze.

Railroaded

At the end of a long and very tiring business meeting an American executive boarded the sleeper train to travel south for his appointment the next day. Sitting relaxing in the bar, he started chatting to a tall and very attractive woman. After much conversation, and several drinks, she invited him back to her berth for a "little nightcap". Eventually, as he had expected, the "little nightcap" turned into a session of love-making and they both retired into the woman's bunk.

When he awoke in the morning the woman was gone and all around him was still and quiet. Jumping out of the bunk he looked out of the window only to discover that the coach he was in had been cut out and left in a remote siding. He turned hurriedly to get dressed only to discover that the woman had stolen all his money and clothes and left him alone, naked and penniless.

1 **railroaded** (AE, slang): abserviert; Wortspiel mit *railroad.*
5 **to chat:** plaudern.
7 **berth:** Schlafwagenbett.
8 **nightcap:** Schlummertrunk.
10 **to retire:** sich zurückziehen.
bunk: Schlafwagenbett.
14 **to be cut out:** abgekoppelt werden.
15 **siding:** Abstellgleis.
17 **penniless:** ohne einen Pfennig in der Tasche.

[Illustration] **headache:** Problem, über das man sich den Kopf zerbricht.

The Substitute

A young girl of sixteen was regularly making love with her boyfriend and, although they were using condoms, she was always scared of becoming pregnant. She would have liked to go on the pill but, as her doctor was also a friend of the family, she was afraid to approach him – an all too familiar story.

One day when tidying the bedrooms at home the girl came across some contraceptive pills belonging to her mother. Thinking that her mother probably did not need them any longer she decided to use them herself. However, just to make sure her mother did not notice, she substituted the contraceptive pills with aspirins.

The pills certainly worked for the girl. However, she was unfortunately caught out a few months later when her mother was found to be pregnant.

4 **to be scared of s.th.:** vor etwas Angst haben.
pregnant: schwanger.
5 **to go on the pill:** die Pille nehmen.
9 **contraceptive pill:** empfängnisverhütende Pille, Anti-Baby-Pille.
12 **to make sure:** sichergehen.

The Dissection

It is common practice for undergraduates at medical school, as part of their anatomy course, to undertake dissections of human corpses. Such dissections are usually made working from the feet upwards. Each week the student would work on a different section of the body and so advance from comparatively easy sections to more complicated ones, such as the head. All undissected sections of the body were kept covered and, at the end of each session, the corpses would be placed in cold storage to await further dissection at a later date. One day, in just such a class, a young man was going through this procedure. However, when the covering was finally drawn back to allow work to commence on the head he looked down and discovered that he had spent the last few months slowly dissecting the body of his late uncle.

1 **dissection:** Sektion (Leichenöffnung im Anatomiekurs des Medizinstudiums).
2 **it is common practice:** es ist allgemein üblich.
7 **comparatively** (adv.): vergleichsweise.
8 f. **undissected:** nicht seziert.
11 **cold storage:** Kühllagerung.
14 **to commence:** anfangen.

The Philanderer's Porsche

A man in California saw an ad in the paper for an "almost new" Porsche, in excellent condition – price $50. He was certain the printers had made a typographical error, but even at $5,000 it would have been a bargain, so he hurried to the address to look at the car.

A nice-looking woman appeared at the front door. Yes, she had placed the ad. The price was indeed $50. "The car," she said, "is in the garage. Come and look at it."

The fellow was overwhelmed. It was a beautiful Porsche, and, as the ad promised, "nearly new." He asked if he could drive the car around the block. The woman said, "Of course," and went with him.

The Porsche drove like a dream. The young man peeled off $50 and handed it over, somewhat sheepishly. The woman gave him the necessary papers, and the car was his.

Finally, the new owner couldn't stand it any longer. He had to know why the woman was selling the Porsche at such a ridiculously low price. Her reply was simple:

1 **philanderer:** Schürzenjäger.
2 **ad:** Kurzform von *advertisement*.
4 f. **typographical error:** Druck-, Satzfehler.
8 **to place an ad:** eine Annonce aufgeben.
10 **overwhelmed:** überwältigt.
14 **drove like a dream:** fuhr sich traumhaft.
15 **to peel off:** hinblättern.
15 f. **sheepishly** (adv.): verlegen.
18 **The new owner couldn't stand it any longer:** Der neue Eigentümer hielt es nicht mehr aus.

With a half-smile on her face, she said, "My husband ran off with his secretary a few days ago and left a note instructing me to sell the car and the house, and send him the money."

1 **half-smile:** angedeutetes Lächeln.

AIDS Mary

As the epidemic of AIDS spreads, so does a story about a mysterious woman who is intentionally giving the disease to others. The story has shown up on the grapevine virtually everywhere, with only minor variations in detail. Here's one telling of it:

A recently divorced man went to a singles bar, where he met a beautiful woman. They became friendly and ended up going to his place, where they made love all night. The man woke up the next morning, and she was gone. He went into the bathroom. Then he looked at the mirror. Scrawled there, in bright red lipstick, was the message, "WELCOME TO THE WORLD OF AIDS!"

3 **intentionally** (adv.): absichtlich.

4 f. **to show up on the grapevine:** gerüchteweise herumgehen, als Gerücht die Runde machen.

12 **to scrawl:** (hin)kritzeln.

A Halloween Party

As the story goes, a married couple is invited to a Halloween costume party, and the wife rents costumes for both of them. On the night of the party, though, she has a severe headache and feels too ill to attend. She urges the husband to go without her, telling him to have a good time, Disappointed, he puts on his costume and leaves, and she takes a couple of aspirin and goes to bed.

But at about nine in the evening, she wakes up without any sign of her headache and decides to attend the party after all. And since her husband hasn't seen her costume, the wife decides to remain incognito and see how he behaves in her absence.

When she arrives at the party, she spots him in his costume, dancing with several different women and openly flirting with them. So the wife, in costume, begins to flirt with her husband. She dances with him and eventually allows him to lead her off to a vacant bedroom where they make love without removing their masks.

Before the midnight unmasking of the guests, the wife slips away and goes home to await the husband's re-

1 **Halloween:** Nacht vom 31. 10. auf den 1. 11., in der böse Geister ihr Unwesen treiben sollen. Wird hauptsächlich in den USA gefeiert. Kinder verkleiden sich und gehen von Haus zu Haus, um Süßigkeiten zu erbetteln.

3 **costume party:** Maskenball.
to rent: hier: ausleihen.

6 f. **to have a good time:** sich gut amüsieren.

15 **to spot:** entdecken.

21 **unmasking:** Demaskierung, Abnehmen der Masken.

turn. She is sitting up in bed reading when he arrives home. He asks her how she is feeling. She says she feels much better now and asks him what kind of time he had at the party.

"Oh, the same old thing," he replies. "I never have much fun when you're not there."

"Did you dance much?"

"No," he says. "In fact, I didn't dance a single dance. I met a few other men who were also there alone, so we went off to the den and played poker. But the guy who borrowed my costume said he had a heck of a good time!"

10 **den:** gemütliches Zimmer (AE).
11 f. **to have a heck of a good time:** sich verdammt gut amüsieren.

The Lover's Telephone Revenge

A man wants to dump his current live-in girlfriend and tells her bluntly one morning that he is going away for two weeks, and he wants her to be gone and to have all of her things cleared out of the apartment when he returns.

When he arrives back home, he half-expects to find the apartment trashed or the girlfriend still there, refusing to leave. Instead, he finds to his satisfaction that the woman and all her possessions are gone, and everything is apparently in order. Then he hears some kind of odd sound coming from the next room and finds the telephone off the hook and a voice spouting some kind of gibberish.

He shrugs and hangs up the receiver, only to learn, when his next phone bill comes, that his former lover had called the time/weather number in Tokyo and left the phone off the hook for a week or so. The bill runs to the thousands of dollars.

2 **to dump s.o.** (infml.): jdn. verlassen, sitzenlassen.
live-in girlfriend: Freundin, mit der man zusammen lebt.
8 **trashed:** in Trümmern.
13 **off the hook:** ausgehängt (Telefon).
to spout: herunterrasseln.
14 **gibberish:** Kauderwelsch.
17 **time/weather number:** telefonische Zeitansage / telefonische Wettervorhersage.
18 f. **to run to s.th.:** sich auf etwas belaufen (Geldsumme).

Editorische Notiz

Die englischen Texte folgen den Sammelausgaben: (1) Jan Harold Brunvand, *The Vanishing Hitchhiker: American Urban Legends and Their Meanings*, New York: Norton, 1981; (2) Jan Harold Brunvand, *Curses! Broiled Again!*, New York / London: Norton, 1990; (3) Paul Smith, *The Book of Nasty Legends*, London: Routledge & Kegan Paul, 1983; dieser Ausgabe sind auch die Illustrationen von David Austin entnommen. Das Glossar erklärt in der Regel alle Wörter, die nicht in *Reclams Englischem Wörterbuch* von Dieter Hamblock (Stuttgart: Reclam, 1996) verzeichnet sind. Die einzelnen Texte sind unabhängig voneinander glossiert.
Unsere Textauswahl ist im folgenden jeweils mit Nummer und Seitenzahl der Sammelausgabe nachgewiesen.

The Persian Cat and the Chihuahua (3) S. 25
The Performing Elephant (3) S. 27
Woodworm-infested Shoes (3) S. 60
The Girl with the Beehive Hairdo (1) S. 65 f.
The Dead Cat in the Package (1) S. 84 f.
The Cat Parcel (1) S. 86 f.
The Snake in the Sweater (1) S. 124 f.
There was this Snake, See ... (1) S. 128 f.
A Bug in the Ear (2) S. 40 f.
Not My Dog (2) S. 116
The Hare Drier (2) S. 151
Dangers of the Microwave Oven II (3) S. 65
Squeaky Canned Cola (3) S. 55
The Perfect Mousse (3) S. 56 f.
The Kentucky Fried Rat (1) S. 70
The Mrs. Fields Cookie Recipe (2) S. 219 ff.
A Mix-up in the Mail (3) S. 106
Tragedy in the Bakery (3) S. 103
Dangers of the Microwave Oven I (3) S. 64
The Minced Butcher (3) S. 26

The Ice-Cream-Cone Caper (2) S. 173
The Grocery Scam (2) S. 247 f.
The Will (2) S. 267
Ornithology (2) S. 277
Trouble with Technology (2) S. 189
The Everlasting Light Bulb (3) S. 67
No Claim (3) S. 78
The Death Car (3) S. 79
The Unstealable Car (2) S. 104
The Unlucky Escape (3) S. 39
The Vanishing Hitchhiker (1) S. 30 f.
The Two Hitchhikers (2) S. 108 f.
The Auto-Pilot (3) S. 63
The Ghost Airliner (1) S. 135
The Second Death (2) S. 67
The Disappearing Room (3) S. 106
The Nude in the RV (1) S. 103
The Dead Scuba Diver (2) S. 47
The Fatal Tee (2) S. 66
The Vanishing Grandmother (3) S. 109
The Hairy-handed Hitchhiker (3) S. 91
The Hook (3) S. 58
The Boyfriend's Death (1) S. 18
The Baby-sitter and the Man Upstairs (1) S. 50–53
The Roommate's Death (1) S. 53 f.
The Graveyard Wager (2) S. 79
Not Your Lucky Night (3) S. 34
Railroaded (3) S. 35
The Substitute (3) S. 46
The Dissection (3) S. 47
The Philanderer's Porsche (1) S. 29 f.
AIDS Mary (2) S. 195
A Halloween Party (2) S. 209 f.
The Lover's Telephone Revenge (2) S. 216

Im Glossar verwendete Abkürzungen

adv.	adverb
aeronaut	aeronautics (Luftfahrt)
AE	American English
arch.	archaic (veraltet)
CE	Canadian English
fig.	figuratively (übertragen)
Fr.	French
infml.	informal (umgangssprachlich)
o.s.	oneself
pl.	plural
prov.	proverbial (sprichwörtlich)
s.o.	someone
s.th.	something

Literaturhinweise

Es sind nur Werke aufgenommen, die im Bibliotheks-Leihverkehr erfahrungsgemäß problemlos zu bekommen sind. Viele der bei Brednich (siehe unten) verzeichneten angloamerikanischen Sammlungen sind nur als Auslands-Fernleihen erhältlich. Die hier aufgeführten Sammlungen enthalten selbst ausführliche wissenschaftliche Bibliographien, so daß auf die Angabe einzelner Artikel verzichtet wurde. Da das Internet eine sich ständig wandelnde Quelle ist, werden Internet-Adressen ebenfalls nicht angeführt. Im Internet empfiehlt sich eine normale Stichwortsuche.

I. *Deutscher Sprachraum*

1. Sammlungen

Brednich, Rolf Wilhelm, *Die Spinne in der Yucca-Palme*, München: Beck, 1990.

– *Die Maus im Jumbo-Jet*, München: Beck, 1991.

– *Das Huhn mit dem Gipsbein*, München: Beck, 1993.

– *Die Ratte am Strohhalm*, München: Beck, 1996.

2. Zeitschrift

Fabula. Zeitschrift für Erzählforschung / Journal of Folktale Studies / Revue d'Etudes sur le Conte Populaire, hrsg. von Rolf Wilhelm Brednich und Hans-Jörg Uther, Universität Göttingen: Seminar für Volkskunde, 1957 ff.

II. *Angloamerikanischer Sprachraum*

1. Sammlungen

Brown, Yorick / Flynn, Mike, *The Best Book of Urban Myths Ever*, London: Carlton, 1998.

Brunvand, Jan Harold, *The Vanishing Hitchhiker: American Urban Legends and Their Meanings*, New York: Norton, 1981.
– *The Choking Doberman*, New York / London: Norton, 1984.
– *The Mexican Pet*, New York / London: Norton, 1986.
– *Curses! Broiled Again!*, New York / London: Norton, 1990.
Smith, Paul, *The Book of Nasty Legends*, London: Routledge & Kegan Paul, 1983.

2. Sammeldarstellungen und Zeitschriften

Bennett, Gillian / Smith, Paul (Hrsg.), *Perspectives on Contemporary Legend*, Bd. 1, Sheffield: Sheffield Academic Press, 1984.
– (Hrsg.), *Perspectives on Contemporary Legend*, Bd. 2, Sheffield: Sheffield Academic Press, 1987.
– (Hrsg.), *Monsters with Iron Teeth. Perspectives on Contemporary Legend*, Bd. 3, Sheffield: Sheffield Academic Press, 1988.
– (Hrsg.), *The Questing Beast. Perspectives on Contemporary Legend*, Bd. 4, Sheffield: Sheffield Academic Press, 1989.
– (Hrsg.), *A Nest of Vipers. Perspectives on Contemporary Legend*, Bd. 5, Sheffield: Sheffield Academic Press, 1990.
– (Hrsg.), *Contemporary Legend: The First Five Years: Abstracts and Bibliographies from the Sheffield Conferences on Contemporary Legend, 1982–1986*, Sheffield: Sheffield Academic Press, 1990.
Contemporary Legend. The Journal of the International Society for Contemporary Legend Research, hrsg. von Joseph P. Goodwin, Muncie (Ind.): 1991 ff.
FOAFtale News, hrsg. von Philip Hiscock, Memorial University of Newfoundland (Canada): Folklore Language Archive, 1985 ff.

Zeitschriften mit dem Stichwort »Folklore« im Titel enthalten ebenfalls häufig Artikel über *urban legends*.